CW01024164

BLOWING BUBBLES

See, the pretty planet!
Floating sphere!
Faintest breeze will fan it
Far or near.
World as light as feather;
Moonshine rays,
Rainbow tints together,
As it plays;
Drooping, sinking, failing,
Nigh to earth,
Mounting, whirling, sailing,
Full of mirth;
Life there, welling, flowing,
Waving round;
Pictures coming, going,
Without sound.
Quick now, be this airy
Globe repell'd!
Never can the fairy
Star be held.
Touch'd--it in a twinkle
Disappears!

By Classic Irish Poet,
William Allingham,
1824 - 1889

Dedicated with much love
to all our Children

CONTRiBUTiONS

Written By
- Jesse Ward -
Phillip Maxwell-Stewart.

Photography - Graphic Design
Christopher Green.

Additional Photography
Clare Mullineux.

Editor
Dulcie Jo-Anne Mauritis.

Story
Simon Maxwell-Stewart.

Illustrator
Monique Pihl.

iNTRODUCTiON

Did you know that bubble solution is one of the top selling children's toys in the world? By the end of the 20th century, 200 million bottles of bubble solution were being sold worldwide every single year!

Most children's delight and engagement with bubbles is immediate. Then, often slowly and tentatively, adults will join them. Creating and blowing bubbles is a shared, communal joy for all ages.

Blowing bubbles is the kind of play that is the physical equivalent of music and poetry. Strange, wonderful, paradoxical; it creates its own magical language!

JOY OF BUBBLES

Most of us have delightful memories of blowing, chasing and popping bubbles. The delicate, ethereal nature of bubbles, their beautiful rainbow tints and their ability to float on a breath of air or a gust of wind, make them a universal joy to children and adults alike.

Bubbles usually last for seconds or minutes but can live for a lifetime in people's memories. Whether blowing or watching, creating or chasing bubbles, we are united across time and space in the unspoken language of wonder.

WHAT IS A BUBBLE?

A bubble is one substance contained in another. This is usually a gas inside a liquid. Soap bubbles are made from a combination of water and soap that has air trapped inside it. When soap and water are mixed together in just the right proportions, air can be blown into the mixture. The liquid will form a thin skin or wall and trap the air, creating a bubble. Soap bubbles are beautiful and can be made in a variety of sizes.

THE SCIENCE BIT

Hydrogen atoms in a water molecule are attracted to oxygen atoms in other water molecules. They 'like' each other and cling together. Even those at the surface of a bubble. This is called 'surface tension' and what makes water appear to have a 'skin'.

Soap molecules are undecided however. Half of them love water, but the other half hates it. When soap molecules are in water, part of them wants to escape. This is why they spread out and cover the whole surface of the water.

Soap, glycerin and sugar slow down the evaporation of water molecules so bubbles can last longer.

HYDROGEN

OXYGEN

HYDROGEN

Can bubbles form in space?

In the vacuum of space, a bubble would not form due to the lack of exterior pressure to counteract the interior pressure within.

WHY BUBBLES LIKE BEING ROUND

If you ask scientists, they will say that bubbles are 'minimal surface structures'.

This means they will always hold the gas or liquid inside of them using the smallest surface area.

The geometric shape with the smallest area for any volume is always a sphere.

WHY BUBBLES POP !

Since bubbles are made from soap and water they can only last as long as the water lasts. In dry air, water evaporates. The water is absorbed by the air around the bubble. As bubbles get old they are prone to pop due to evaporation. Also gravity pulls the water molecules to the bottom of the bubble, making the upper half of the bubble increasingly thinner. This causes the skin of the bubble to get thinner and thinner until it finally pops!

Evaporation isn't the only reason that bubbles pop. Sometimes dry objects can pop them. When a bubble floats through the air and lands on your finger, or on a blade of dry grass, or the wall of your house, the bubble will probably pop. Most dry and absorbent materials will poke a hole in the bubble skin, allowing the air to escape making the bubble disappear. On the other hand, if your bubble lands on water, any wet surface or natural materials (such as cotton or hair) it is likely to gently come to a rest or bounce back in to the air. You can can try catching or bouncing bubbles on a cotton tea towel.

RAINBOWS IN BUBBLES

White light is actually lots of different colours all at once. Bubbles are very special in that they can show these colours individually. When light hits a bubble, some of it bounces off the front of the film and some of it bounces off the back film. Different thicknesses of bubbles will show us different colours.

When you first blow a bubble, you will probably see green and blue, then magenta or purple. Then just before the bubble pops, most of it will become a dark, golden yellow or almost black. Sometimes the surface of the bubble is very thin in some parts and thicker in others. When that happens you will see many different colours on the bubble all at once, making it appear like a rainbow.

iNGREDiENTS

WATER is the main ingredient required to make bubble solution. Water varies in what is referred to as 'hard' and 'soft' water. A quick Internet search will let you know what type of water is in your area. Soft water is the best type of water to make bubbles. You can buy water softeners. Some Bubbleologists buy soft bottled water for performing. Having said this, it is still possible to make wonderful bubbles using all types of water.

DETERGENT is the second most important ingredient and it is found in your everyday washing-up liquid. Adding detergent will make the bubbles bubble! It lowers the surface tension of the water to actually make a bubble. Double check the back of the bottle. The ingredients should say 15-30% anionic surfactant. This is the active ingredient. Washing up liquids of the same brand can have different anionic percentages.

By using just these two ingredients (water and detergent) you can make quite good, small bubbles. But to really get to grips with your bubble tricks you will need to add a couple of extra ingredients.

 GLYCERIN stops the water evaporating from the film around the bubble and helps the bubble live for longer.

 BAKING POWDER makes the mixture stable.

BUBBLE FORMULAS

You will need: -
A set of measuring spoons. A big mixing bowl. A measuring jug.
A plastic spoon.

Ingredients:

1ml glycerin (or about 5 or 6 drops).
45ml detergent (about 3 tablespoons)
750ml warm water.
1/4 x teaspoon of baking powder

Mix the glycerin and the detergent together in the mixing bowl. Make sure you don't stir too vigorously as you don't want too much foam. Whilst stirring slowly, add the warm water to the bowl. Warm water will help the ingredients to dissolve.

Once it's all mixed together, sprinkle the baking powder evenly over the top. This bit is fun! The mixture might fizz as the baking powder is added to the water. An even covering is important or else there is a tendency for the formula to clump.

The temperature of the solution can have an effect on the life of a bubble. The warmer the solution – the thinner the bubble. A thin bubble will drain faster and dry out more quickly.

A little trick is to put the solution in the freezer or refrigerator for a short time to slow down the process of evaporation.

Many people randomly add more soap liquid, thinking that the bubble solution will be superior. This is not true; too much soap liquid will reduce the elasticity of the bubble skin. If you wish to experiment, it's best to make small, calculated changes to your formula.

Most Bubbleologists have created their own secret formulas by constant experimenting. Other commonly added ingredients include clear honey, icing sugar and surgical lubricants. If you do add sugar or honey, we suggest adding just under 1/2 teaspoon to your mixture.

BUBBLING TIPS

Find a good place for bubble blowing. If you're making bubbles indoors, you'll need some absorbent material on the floor to prevent it from becoming slippery. You'll also need a good supply of cloth or paper towels to clean up spills.

Bubble solution can sting if it gets in your eyes. If this happens, carefully rinse your eyes with water immediately.

Have a clean washcloth and warm water handy for rinsing any burst bubbles that may come in contact with the eyes.

CLEAN UP

When you've finished making bubbles, you can use paper towels to wipe up as much of the bubble solution as you can from tables and floors.

Don't use water to clean up the leftover solution as you'll make a foamy mess! Instead, use a little white vinegar.

HAND BUBBLES

You can buy or make many different kinds of wands. However, you don't need to make or buy anything in order to create bubbles (well, except for the solution). You can start with the simplest fun device of all, your own hands!

Small Hand Bubbles

Dip your whole hand into a bucket of bubble mixture. Then touch your thumb to the palm of your hand.

Slowly run the tip of your thumb up along your index finger right to the top. You should be able to see a film form inside your hand. Lift your hand a few inches from your mouth and gently blow.

Blowing quickly will give you lots of small bubbles, whilst blowing slowly will enable you to blow much larger bubbles.

BIG HAND BUBBLES

Use both hands to form a circle touching your thumbs and forefingers together, making sure your entire hands and wrists are fully submerged in your bubble liquid.

Slowly lift your hands out of the solution – you should see a film between your hands. Blow through this film to create bubbles.

If your hands are still wet you will be able to catch, hold and manipulate any bubbles you make.

This includes cutting bubbles, blowing bubbles inside bubbles, and even joining two or more bubbles into one.

MOVING BUBBLES AROUND

Bubbles float because both the bubble and the air trapped inside it are very light. A bubble hitches a ride on the slightest breeze. All solids, gases and liquids are made of molecules. Density refers to how tightly packed the molecules are. The warmer the air, the less packed or dense the molecules become.

Warm air always rises. This is how a hot air balloon flies. When the sun heats the ground, in turn this will heat the air which in turn will rise. This being the case up, up and away the bubble will float. When bubbles are blown indoors, where the air is very still, the bubbles are likely to settle on a surface and pop.

There are three basic ways in which to move a bubble.

The first is to blow the bubble in the direction you wish to move it.

The second way of moving bubbles involves air density. Hold a book or a stiff piece of card so that its flat surface is close to the bubble. Quickly move the book or card away from the bubble. The air behind the book or card will become less dense, and the bubble will move in its wake. This is the best way to stop a bubble from hitting the floor if it's too tricky or difficult to blow from underneath it. When placing the card or book close to the bubble, make sure you're not accidentally fanning it.

The third way to move a bubble is to attach it to a wet wand or soapy hand. Carry the bubble to your preferred location, and with an upward jerk, relaunch it into the air or blow it off your hand.

Combining all three techniques, see how long you can keep a bubble from hitting the ground.

BUBBLE WANDS

Bubble wands come in a wide variety of shapes and sizes, and may not be wand-like at all. A variety of commercial, professional and common household materials can be used to create bubbles from tiny to whale-sized!

Commercial Bubble Wands

Commercially made wands can be the simple traditional plastic ones that come in bottles of bubble solution. These wands are too small to do most tricks. The ridges on plastic wands are designed to hold more bubble mixture so they can last for longer. The larger the bubble wand, the more mixture it needs to hold.

Commercial wands come in many designs and sizes. Some have a smaller wand inside a larger, outer wand. These special designs will allow you to blow bubbles inside bubbles. Others are large wands with lots of small wands attached to the outer perimeter. These are great for blowing different sized bubbles at the same time. Use the larger wands by waving them slowly or hold them up to the wind.

Professional Bubble Wands

Professionals tend to either make their own wands or use expensive wands made by high-end prop makers. Some of these have a cotton cover on an aluminium hoop which can be made to various diameters. These are perfect for putting people in giant bubbles and for large stage shows.

A professional wand should always have just the right amount of ridges or material to hold the perfect amount of liquid in relation to its size. Some wands have no ridges at all and are used for tricks which do not require much liquid.

Customised wands can be made out of acrylic or Perspex. They are clear so that the audience focuses on the trick and the bubbles it is creating, instead of the wand. This adds a touch of gentle magic to the show.

Wands can be customised and made to enhance or to go with any professional Bubbleologist's personal colour scheme or theme.

SMALL WAND CONTROL

Using a small wand is all about control; controlling the pressure of the breath released from your mouth, controlling where you aim the stream of air released from your mouth, and controlling the distance between your mouth and the wand you hold in your hand.

If you experiment with these three points of control then you will find the best place to blow and how hard to blow to create either loads of small bubbles or big bubbles at will. The slower you blow, the bigger the bubble…but watch out not to blow too slowly or you won't get a bubble at all!

Wrong

Most people would naturally hold the wand this way. Holding the wand this way up means much of the bubble mixture is going to drip down onto your fingers, wasting most of it and getting your fingers wet.

Correct

Holding the wand this way causes the mixture to run down the wand, saving a mess and also making sure you get the most from it. Make sure your wand is wet right to the end! If you are blowing large bubbles, flick the wand up to give the bubbles added lift when releasing them.

BUBBLES USING A 2ND WAND

Once you have achieved the skill of blowing some fairly big bubbles with just one wand, you might find that the bubble gets too big and that gravity takes over, pulling the bubble off the wand.

You can use a second wand to counteract gravity. Dip the second wand into your mixture, making sure it is as wet as possible, and gently touch the top of your bubble. This will both add more liquid to the bubble as well as support its weight.

When releasing your bubble, give your hands an upward flick. A falling bubble can always be caught by a wet wand or soapy hands.

There are many fun bubble sculptures and exciting tricks that can be performed with held bubbles.

HOMEMADE WANDS

Making your own bubble wands can be a great project for children and parents. Even many professional Bubbleologists prefer to make their own wands. Most people find that homemade bubble wands (including those featured in this book) work better than many non-professional, standard, commercial wands and can often be less expensive!

Homemade bubble wands can be made from just about anything!

Marvellous wands can be made from drinking straws, string, wire hangers, party plates and cups and pipe cleaners.

Pipe Cleaner Wands

 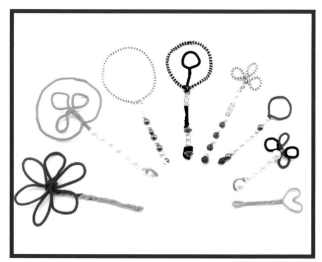

A single pipe cleaner is perfect to make a basic wand.

Two pipe cleaners can be twisted together to make a larger pipe cleaner wand.	An inner wand could be added using a third pipe cleaner.	A fourth pipe cleaner can then be used to reinforce the handle.

This will enable you to blow bubbles inside bubbles. These wands will need to be gently waved through the air.

Please note when blowing with your mouth it is very difficult to blow the inner and outer wands at the same time.

Trumpet Wands

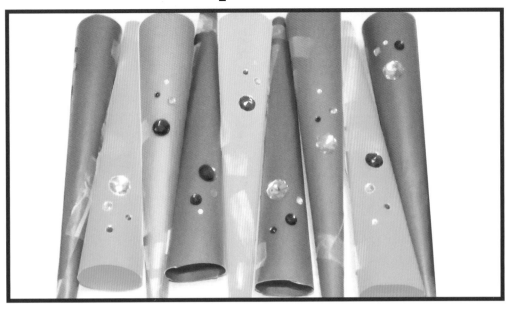

You can use brightly coloured card rolled into a cone shape to make trumpet wands. For everyday use, cereal boxes work well. Tape the joining edges and trim both ends to make them even. Make sure you roll the smaller end with a large enough opening to blow through. Children can decorate their wands with stick-on crystals or other materials if they wish. Trumpet wands are very easy to construct. They make great bubbles and are a big hit with both children and adults!

When trimming the ends of trumpet wands, they can easily crush. If this happens, cut one cone shape out and use this as a template for the others.

These wands are particularly good for football sized bubbles and bubble domes.

BUBBLES INSIDE BUBBLES

Although this is one of the most visually impressive tricks, it also happens to be one of the easiest to accomplish.

The easiest way to blow a bubble inside a bubble is to catch a big bubble on a big bubble wand first! If you want a bubble about the size of a football, a wand about the same size will be perfect.

Make a few bubbles and choose one to catch. You will want to catch this bubble underneath your bubble wand.

Once you have caught a bubble, just take your time to have a good look at it.

Watch the mixture and the colour swirl around. You might notice that a lot of the mixture is pooling towards the bottom of the bubble.

If there is a lot of frothy mixture, either choose a different bubble or, using a wet straw, carefully cut the drip off the bottom of the bubble.

Tip! The second bubble is usually better than the first, especially if your mixture is a little foamy.

How to Blow

Purse your lips as if to blow a bubble.

Using a short, sharp blast of air, you can blow a bubble into another bubble.

Some people like to say "Pa" or "Po" or even "Pop" while they do this, but remember to keep your lips pursed as you say it.

Where to Blow

To blow a bubble inside a bubble, the best place to blow is upwards from the bottom of the bubble.

This is where the bubble is thickest so you will be using the mixture from the strongest part of the bubble.

When your technique is perfect try using a wand to hold the larger bubble. Purposefully pop the film inside your wand and watch as the air inside the bubble escapes, taking all your little bubbles with it like a bubble volcano! Whoosh! It is also possible to pop the inner bubble(s) by poking a soapy straw through the outer bubble, and inserting a dry stick through the straw and poking the inner bubbles you wish to pop.

WEATHER

INDOORS or OUTDOORS?

The best place for small, intricate bubble sculptures is indoors. The best place for large bubbles and garlands and nets is outdoors, although preferably not on very hot, sunny days.

Please bear in mind that even though the bubbles won't do as well from a professional Bubbleologist's point of view, you can still have amazing bubble fun on a hot summer's day! Bring a picnic, some bubble solution, and a selection of wands, and create a magical day of bubble experiences!

This weather chart shows you the best days to practise Bubbleology. Bubbles love humidity, so days that are foggy, or right after a rain storm are best.

Direct sunlight can lessen the life of a bubble due to evaporation. On drier days, you can spray the air with a mist if you are performing longer bubble tricks.

	PERFECT	OK	POOR
Warm & Sticky	✓	☐	☐
After Rain	✓	☐	☐
Cloudy Day	☐	✓	☐
Light Rain	☐	✓	☐
Really Cold	☐	☐	✗
Hot & Dry	☐	☐	✗

GiANT BUBBLES

Tri-string wands are perfect for making giant bubbles. Playing outside with super-sized bubbles can be a universally enjoyable activity for all ages. What better fun is there than watching the bubbles you create float with the breeze?

Giant bubbles are one of the most fascinating elements of Bubbleology, and surprisingly, one of the easiest!

TRI - STRING WANDS

A Tri-String is made up of two sticks and two lengths of absorbent rope or string. One length of rope needs to be twice as long as the other. The shorter length will be the top rope, and the longer length will be the bottom rope.

Attach the ends of the ropes to the end of the sticks as per the diagram, making sure that the ropes overlap at the point that they attach.

Find a sturdy container or bucket to pour your bubble solution into. With your back to the breeze, dip the string into your bucket of bubble mixture. Don't stir it around. Dip it straight in and straight out.

When you lift the string out, keep the ends of the sticks together. This ensures that you don't open the Tri-String too soon.

Absorbent Rope

Make sure rope overlaps where joined.

Bottom string twice as long as top string.

Hand Sticks

Let any excess mixture drip back into the bucket.

Tri-Strings can be made in any size, from rods as little as 30 to 40 cms with string lengths of 40 to 60 cms, all the way up to using giant fishing poles and rope of six to ten metres long!

Please note that the larger the Tri-String, the thicker the rope or string has to be in order to supply enough bubble solution liquid for the increasingly larger bubbles.

When you are making bubbles outside, you need to think about the weather and the direction of the wind. You want the wind to be blowing on your back so that the bubbles fly off the string in front of you. In very hot weather, bubbles don't work as well because the water evaporates really quickly and they pop.

Open the Tri-String slowly so that you can judge how fast the wind is blowing. If it's blowing briskly, don't open the string very far.

If it's a nice, still day you will be able to open the Tri-String to its full length at the top string.

If, at this point you have opened the Tri-String and the wind isn't blowing the film into a bubble, you may need to move the sticks to capture the air inside the bubble. This has to be done in a smooth motion which is not too fast or you will pop the film.

To make a complete bubble, you will need to close it. Bring the ends of the sticks back together. Try to do this smoothly; not too quickly or too slowly.

Always dispose of unused bubble liquid responsibly. Please don't throw it on to flower beds or into ponds. Please save it for future use.

GARLAND

A Bubble Garland is a fantastic prop for creating multiple bubbles of various sizes simultaneously. Cotton rope is an absorbent material and ideal for garlands.

For the poles you can use anything from bamboo canes from a garden centre to fishing rods.

Tie at Intervals

Hand Sticks

To make a Garland, get two lengths of rope, one at least twice as long as the other. Tie or sew the bottom string to the top string at intervals making loops – please refer to diagram.

The size of the bubbles you make will vary depending on the size of the loops in the garland. Attach one end of the Garland to each of your rods.

Dip your garland into a bucket of bubble solution and lift it out. Point the rods outwards and up into the air with your back to the wind. Either let the wind create thousands of bubbles or wave the garland through the air.

BUBBLE NET

The Bubble Net is quite literally a net tied to two poles or sticks. This gives off a slightly different effect to the Garland, creating a wall of bubbles. Again, it's a truly magnificent sight to see!

BUBBLE CHAIN

There are two main ways to make a Bubble Chain. Both involve using a straw (or a pen with the inside removed) and require precise, slow hand movements.

Safety Tip – be sure not to suck the mixture through the straw.

Before you start to make a Bubble Chain, you will need to practice blowing a bubble onto a wand using a straw. Dip both the wand and the straw into the mixture to ensure there are no dry places on which to pop your bubble.

Hold the wand horizontally, and then touch the wet end of the straw underneath the wand. Start to blow slowly through the straw. Your bubble should hang down from the wand.

Sometimes your bubble might stay stuck to the straw when you try to pull the straw away. Use a slight downward flick to release the bubble from the straw.

Look carefully at the bubble you have just created. Does it look like it's about to drip from the bottom? If so, then there is too much mixture in it. Take your wet straw and touch it to the bottom of the bubble at an angle. This will make the extra mixture drip down the straw and away from the bubble without popping it.

Once you have practised this a few times you will be ready to try adding another bubble.

Make your first bubble on the wand, and then touch your straw to the bottom of this bubble.

Blow slowly through your straw to produce another bubble. Remember your downward flick to release the straw from the bubble.

Congratulations! You have made your first bubble chain! Now you can continue to add bubbles to the bottom of the chain until it pops or gravity takes over. The more you practice, the longer your chain will get!

BOUNCING BUBBLES

Most bubbles will bounce if they hit a suitable surface. Bubbles generally bounce better on cotton and wool. If you want to make your bubbles extra bouncy and durable, we recommend the solution below:

Bouncing Bubble Solution:

2 packages of vegetarian gelatin
1 Litre of water, freshly boiled
59ml or 4 tablespoons glycerin
59ml or 4 tablespoons detergent

This next part you will need to do with adult supervision. Dissolve the gelatin in the boiled water, and then add the soap detergent and glycerin. Leave the mixture for five or ten minutes to cool to room temperature. When it goes cold you will need to reheat the mixture to use it as the gelatin will clump and need to melt again.

If you have a big bubble wand with a large diameter, you can bounce a bubble on the film surface, rather like you would a tennis racket and tennis ball.

You can also bounce a bubble on your bubble wand or any other soapy-covered prop.

The Bouncing Bubbles World Record is 195! This record was achieved by Kuo-Sheng Lin of Taiwan in 2012. He wore a glove on his hand to assist with the bouncing.

A bubble's shell is composed of a layer of water molecules surrounded by two thin layers of soap. A bubble will freeze below 0 degrees centigrade, like all water. As ice crystals form in the bubble's surface, cracks form along with them. This means that any air trapped inside the sphere suddenly has an escape route. Frozen bubbles, when removed from the outdoors or the freezer, won't last long, so enjoy their beauty in the moment!

FROZEN BUBBLES

Mix up a batch of bubble solution and blow individual bubbles onto a soapy, wet plate.

Blowing bubbles with a plastic straw rather than a wand will create better results.

Place in the freezer for about 30 minutes, or outside if the temperature is below zero.

Be patient, it may take a number of tries before you'll have one that freezes successfully.

The crystals and etchings in the bubble skin are simply spellbinding!

What sort of shapes can you see?

FOAM

When transporting your liquid, pouring it and dipping your bubble equipment, try to create as little foam as possible. It helps to have a second container in which to keep unwanted foam. A small tea strainer can be perfect for removing foam. Foam prevents a film forming on your bubble-blowing apparatus. That said, foam in itself can be great fun when not combined with standard Bubbleology.

Foamy Fun

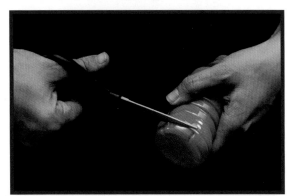

Making a foam tube called a Bubble Snake is a great, easy activity for children! All you need is an empty water bottle with the bottom removed, a piece of cloth, and an elastic band!

Oh, and don't forget the bubble mixture!

Cut off the bottom end of a water bottle with a pair of scissors.

Cut the cloth so that it's bigger than the bottom of the bottle. Hold the cloth so it's covering the bottom of the bottle and fasten it in place with an elastic band.

The smaller the bottle, the easier it will be to blow, but larger ones can be used for extra thick bubble snakes.

Dip the clothed end of the bubble bottle into the bubble mixture. Lift it up and now simply blow through the cap end.

Coloured Foam

Using a different colour for each container, add five to ten drops of non-toxic, easily washable food colouring to each and gently stir. Various colours can be slowly mixed together to create swirls of multi-coloured foam.

You can also make swirly, rainbow-like multi-coloured bubble foam snakes. Just add a few drops of food colouring to the cloth before dipping your bubble snake wand into the bubble mixture! how long a foam snake you can make?

Practice writing your name or drawing a foam picture on the floor or table.

BUBBLES WITH EVERYDAY OBJECTS

Bubbles can be blown using just about anything with a hole in it!

Here are some suggestions to get you started:

A colander. This will make hundreds of tiny bubbles!

A badminton or tennis racket.
Buy a cheap one from a discount store.

Both of these will create lots of small and medium bubbles joined together.

Regular drinking straw or a pen with the inside removed.

A cardboard tube.

A rolled-up piece of paper.

With the following two items you will need to get your hands wet with mixture so you don't pop the bubbles:

Charity wristbands are perfect for making bubbles!

The plastic loops which hold a six pack of cans or bottles together.

Have a search around your house and see what you can find.

BUBBLE GUNS & MACHINES

Double guns have an inner and outer wand enabling them to blow bubbles inside bubbles.

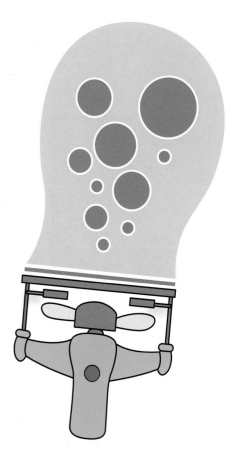

The standard Bubble Gun pumps the soapy liquid to the top of the wand and a fan blows air through the wand's hole.

Water shooting Bubble Guns blow bubbles and have a water shooting spout feature which enables you to hone your firing skills on the bubbles you've just created!

As you can see from these pictures, bubble guns and bubble blowing machines are great fun. An ideal way to create lots and lots of bubbles at once. Excellent for bubble parties or a bubble session in the local park.

JOINING 2 BUBBLES

Two bubbles can actually join together to make one large bubble, rather than just sticking to each other. The trick to this is making them hit each other in the thinnest part of the bubble forcing them to join together and share the same air.

Make two bubbles of equal size. Catch the bubbles on medium size wands or use soapy hands. Position your wands or hands above the bubbles.

Hold them close together but not touching. Pull the bubbles upwards (this will make the bubble skin thinner) and collide the bubbles together at the point where they meet their wands.

Hopefully the two bubbles have now become one. Don't worry if the bubbles don't stick together. Practice makes perfect and it can take a few tries to get this right.

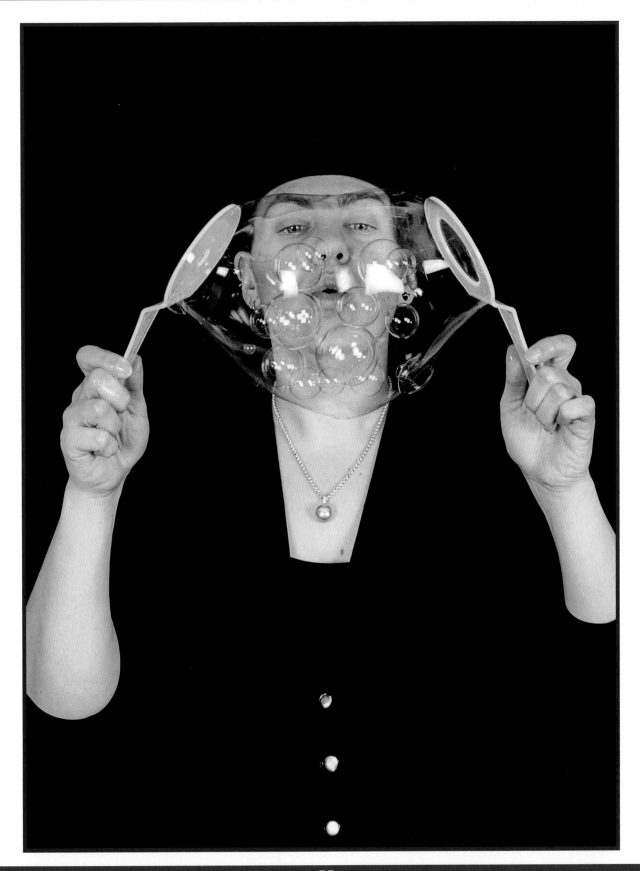

SPLITTING BUBBLES

The most common technique for splitting a bubble is blowing across its surface.

To do this, blow as hard as you can very close to the bubble's edge. You should blow above the bubble and not below it. New bubbles will curl and form, creating lots of smaller bubbles! You can continue splitting bubbles in this way, making more and more smaller bubbles. Blowing a bubble inside a bubble is another way of splitting bubbles.

USING A WAND

Another interesting way to cut a bubble in half is using a soapy wand or cane.

Blow yourself a medium sized bubble about the size of a miniature football.
Then, using your wet wand or cane (make sure it is completely wet), slice the bubble in half. You will need to try a few times to get the speed just right. If you go too slowly you may just pass your stick through the bubble.

If you go a bit faster but still too slowly, you will find you have created two bubbles stuck together. With just the right speed you will have two completely separate bubbles flying away from each other. However, if you are too fast, one or both of your bubbles may pop.

DOME FLOWERS

Find yourself a nice, flat, plastic plate and a straw.

Make sure that the plate is completely wet with bubble mixture.

Now touch your straw to the plate making sure it is at an angle rather than straight down.

Blow slowly through your straw to produce a bubble dome.

Try to blow the biggest bubble dome you can make!

Blow smaller bubble domes all around the edge of your big bubble dome.

Try creating lovely patterns like a flower. A flower consists of an outer edge of six or more same sized bubble domes with one larger dome in the middle.

A further row can be added to the top. The possibilities are endless.

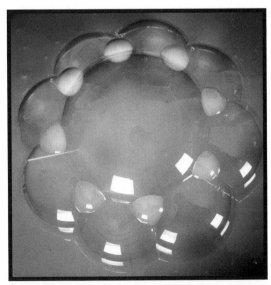

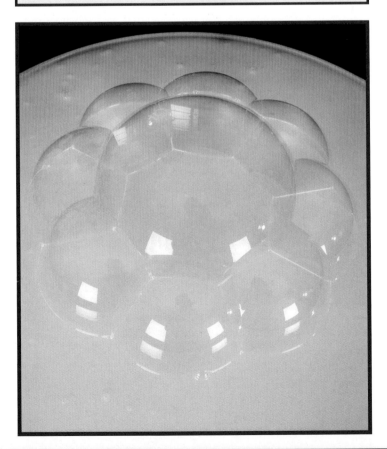

See how many domes inside a dome you can make!

Now that you have had fun experimenting and playing with some of the easier Bubble Dome tricks, try to blow a Bubble Dome inside another Bubble Dome. Again, make sure both your plate and bubble straw are wet with mixture.

The most soap bubble domes created inside one another is 15! This was achieved by Chung-Tai Su (Taiwan) on 26th April, 2012. He used a large tube to blow a huge bubble dome and then smaller tubes to blow individual bubble domes inside it.

Try to blow your first bubble dome to a medium size as this will expand once you put another one inside it. Once you have your first Bubble Dome, place your straw back inside it. Again at an angle, blow your second bubble dome inside the first. When you are pulling your straw out of the bubble, pull it out from the top without moving the bubble.

Play around with where you start blowing your bubble to get the second bubble in the very centre of the first bubble. This may take a little practice to achieve consistency! Once you are consistently blowing the second bubble in the centre of the first, it's time to try the third bubble.

At this point, if you pull your straw out of the side of both the second bubble and the first, you will find that the second bubble will get pulled to the outside of the first one.

Now blow your third bubble in the same way you did bubbles one and two.

Try to remove the straw without making the bubble move around on the plate. To prevent this from happening, lift your straw out of the top and centre of both bubbles. This is important to practice if you want to make multiple bubble domes inside each other.

INVISIBLE BUBBLE

This trick is particularly effective and magical when using a volunteer. Dip a large bubble wand into the solution. Show the audience the bubble film by gently blowing so that they can see its rippling effect without actually creating a bubble.

Now ask your volunteer to put their hand through the bubble film. It will immediately pop. Re-dip the bubble wand to make a new film, and ask your volunteer to fully submerge their hand and lower arm into the bubble mixture. Next, have them push their hand through the film, fingertips first. They will now have their hand all the way through the bubble film without having popped it! This is a special moment in itself! Now ask the volunteer to make a claw shape with their hand, as if they were holding an invisible bubble. Keeping their hand in this same claw position, have them pull it out of the wand! They are now holding an actual bubble! This is a very magical moment and appears to be impossible!

At this point, ask your volunteer to open their hand and gently blow their magic bubble into the air!

BUBBLE CUBE

When two bubbles of equal volume join together, their connecting walls will become flat due to equal pressure from both sides. By blowing a bubble in the middle of six other bubbles (two vertical, four horizontal), the middle bubble will have equal pressure from six sides, creating an inner cube.

If you think of shapes three-dimensionally, then you can make any geometric shape. A cube has six sides three-dimensionally. A bubble cube is made up of seven bubbles! There are six around the outside and one cubic one in the middle.

Have you practised your Bubble Chain?
If so, you are now ready to make a Bubble Cube.

1. Blow one bubble that stays attached to your wand. Start as if you are blowing a chain, but make it a chain of two equal sized bubbles.

2. Now, take a straw that has been dipped in your bubble solution and use this to blow another bubble at the bottom of the first bubble.

3. Where the two bubbles attach, you will need to blow four evenly sized bubbles.

4. You might have to re-dip your straw in your solution from time to time.

5. Make sure that the four bubbles go all the way around so that the first bubble blown is attached to the fourth bubble blown.

6. If you have done this correctly, you will see a small cube appear in the centre of these bubbles.

7. Now take your straw, and go inside the bubble, until it touches the cube. Blow very gently to expand the size of the inner cube

DODECAHEDRON

A dodecahedron is a 12-sided shape.

This bubble was invented and explored by the Bubble Master, Tom Noddy.

A dodecahedron is very similar to a cube in its construction, but takes a lot more skill and patience to get right. The construction needs to be completed before the bubbles dry out, and it's harder to keep the bubbles in the right place.

Start to construct the bubble the same way you did for the cube. As with the bubble cube, start placing bubbles around the centre edge where the bubbles meet.

You will need to make a row of five bubbles of the same size.

Once you have done this, you need to make another row of five bubbles below the first.

Remember to re-dip your wand or straw approximately every three bubbles.

Insert your wet straw in to the centre of the sculpture and inflate the inner dodecahedron

CAROUSEL

Once you have mastered the Bubble Cube you can try your hand at the more intricate Bubble Carousel.

The Bubble Carousel is a beautiful bubble. In fact, it's one of Bubbleologist Jesse's favourite bubbles!

This bubble is constructed in a very similar way to the Bubble Cube.

You will need a bubble wand and a straw.

The first two bubbles are the same as for the Bubble Cube, and should be the same size.

For the third bubble, place your straw at the join where bubbles number one and two meet. Blow bubble number three to less than a quarter or the size of bubbles one and two.

To release bubble three, flick it sideways along the join of bubbles one and two so that it spins around the outside of the structure. You will need to use this same technique for the rest of the bubbles, flicking them around the join so they collide with the other smaller bubbles and join up.

Once you get to the last bubble, you may need to help it join up with the first smaller bubble by moving the straw in that direction before releasing. It will probably take a few tries to get to this point, but don't give up! What you are about to achieve is magical!

At this point make sure your wand is wet again. Place the end of the wand into the middle of bubbles one and two, going in through a join. Slowly blow into this flat octagon
(depending on how many outside ring bubbles you made, of course).

Take your straw out nice and slowly and point it away from your bubble sculpture. Now blow as hard as you can to make sure there is no bubble film or liquid left in the straw.

Next point your straw at the edge of the small ring of bubbles and blow. This should send them spinning around the centre, creating a moving piece of art.

PEOPLE IN BUBBLES

Bubbleologists around the world have specially made bubble equipment to make human sized bubbles, but this method uses common household objects that are easy to find.

To put a person in a bubble you need a LOT of bubble mixture,
a small paddling pool and a hula hoop.

The hula hoop should be wrapped in cotton. Old cut-up cotton sheets work perfectly for this purpose, or thick cotton string.

Fill the paddling pool with cold big bubble mixture, about an inch or two deep. It should be deep enough to completely submerge the hula hoop in the mixture.

Ask the person to stand in the centre of the pool. They will probably want to take off their shoes and socks, or wear clean wellies. Alternatively, you could place a small stool in the middle of the paddling pool. Please make sure they are very careful getting in and out of the pool as it will be very slippery!

Making sure your hands are wet with mixture, lift the hoop straight up over the top of the person's head. This will work much better indoors or on a very still day. If you are going to do it indoors, make sure you have lots of towels ready to clean up any splashes. When the hula hoop is over the person's head, twist the hoop while still slowly lifting to shut the bubble.

Make sure the edges of the paddling pool are completely wet with mixture so your bubble doesn't pop prematurely. As always, remember that any dry surface will always pop a bubble!

BUBBLE INSIDE A BUBBLE INSIDE A BUBBLE

You'll need three different sized wands for this trick. Make sure your fingers, wands and straw are fully soaked in bubble solution before you start. The key to this trick is holding the wands still and using very gentle movements with the straw. Using your largest wand make a football sized bubble – flick it off the wand and catch it again. Carefully insert the medium sized wand and straw through the film of the first bubble. Blow a slightly smaller bubble through the straw on to the inner wand. Now place the third, smallest wand and the straw through the film of the first and second bubbles. You'll need to use one hand to hold all three wands here. Gently blow the third bubble through the straw and onto the inner wand. You now have a bubble inside a bubble inside a bubble.

BUBBLE CUBE INSIDE A BUBBLE

Ensure your straw and wand have been fully submerged in bubble solution before attempting this trick. You'll need two wands of different sizes. Use the shorter wand to blow a football size bubble. Then insert the second wand and straw and begin making the Cubic Bubble sculpture as explained earlier in this book.

Tip! Practise making a really small bubble cube sculpture first.

SOME HISTORY

The earliest paintings of children playing with bubbles appeared in the 17th century when Flemish painters showed children blowing bubbles with clay pipes.

In the 19th century, London's A. & F. Pears created a famous advertising campaign for its soaps using a painting by John Everett Millais of a child playing with bubbles. (This painting is below)

Generations of 18th and 19th century mothers gave their children their leftover washing soap to blow bubbles. At the beginning of the 20th century, street peddlers were among the first to sell bubbles as a toy.

Even though children have been blowing bubbles as entertainment for over 400 years, the birth place of the bubble solution we all know of today, is actually Chicago, in the USA. Chemtoy, a cleaning supplies company based in that city, began selling the soapy solution in the 1940s, helping spark the bubble blowing craze that is still going strong today.

'Boy Blowing
Bubbles',
Edouard Manet,
1869

'Bubbles',
Sir John Everett
Millais,
1886

'Two Boys Blowing
Bubbles',
Adriaen Hanneman ,
1630

SOME FACTS

Blowing bubbles can be used for therapeutic purposes. The pursed lip kind of breathing which is used to blow bubbles increases pressure on the airways, which helps keep them open. When you exhale using pursed lips, you use most of the air in your lungs which leaves more room for new, freshly inhaled air. This helps to give improved circulation to the respiratory system which is a benefit to both emotional and physical well-being. A favourite breathing game during chest physiotherapy sessions for children with cystic fibrosis is blowing bubbles through an "O" shaped mouth. This has also been used in speech therapy too.

Research in Switzerland has shown that blowing bubbles for entertainment purposes of young children has a positive effect in the region of the child's brain that controls motor skills.

For more information about Jesse Ward, our fabulous featured Bubbleologist, please go to: www.bubbleplay.co.uk

This book has been produced in conjunction with Indy Bubbles, which make the world famous Indy Bubble concentrates.

professionalbubbleology.com

Visit our website.
Please share with us any photos, unique tricks you have created, anecdotes, funny stories ... in fact anything at all you wish to share with the bubble world! You never know, with your permission, you might be included in future editions of this book!

You can't look at a bubble and feel angry !

HONEY COMB RECIPE

Butter, for greasing, 200g caster sugar
5 tbsp golden syrup, 2 tsp bicarbonate of soda

Grease a 20cm square tin with the butter.

Mix the caster sugar and syrup in a deep saucepan and stir over a gentle heat until the sugar has melted.

Try not to let the mixture bubble until the sugar grains have disappeared. Once completely melted, turn up the heat a little and simmer until you have an amber coloured caramel (this won't take long), then as quickly as you can turn off the heat, tip in the bicarbonate and beat in with a wooden spoon until it has all disappeared and the mixture is foaming.

Scrape into the tin immediately but be careful as the mixture will be very hot.

The mixture will continue bubbling in the tin, simply leave it and in about 1hr - 1hr 30mins the honeycomb will be hard and ready to crumble or snap into chunks.

Global Bubble Parade

Every year, there is a global celebration of bubble creation called the Global Bubble Parade. Over 100,000 people from 60 different countries hold enormous bubble themed parties that anyone and everyone is invited to attend. The organisers of this event have one simple belief –that happiness and emotional well-being are vital to our lives, and what better way to achieve this than through bubbles. The event has caused so much global happiness that it was even awarded a European Peace Prize. Why not found out where your nearest parade is, or see if you can host your own in your city?

http://bubbleparade.org/

A DAY IN THE LIFE OF MICHAEL BUBBLE...

A most remarkable thing happened today. I was born! It all took place in such a flurry of activity that I scarcely knew what was happening. What I do remember is the first sight I ever saw, and that was the delightful face of the young girl who breathed life into my siblings and me.

I do wish I'd had the time to stop and thank her for bringing me into this world, but before I knew it, I was off and away astride a gust of wind. I floated far away from that garden with its swings and slides and comfortable rocking chairs, drifting into the unknown.

I had begun my life with all my family around me. It gave me a warm, comforting feeling to know that they were there beside me, just as new and shiny and round as me. But I soon noticed that our numbers were thinning. One by one they were popping! Though I yelled at them to "Watch out for that branch!", "Steer away from the chimney!", "Rise above that sharp fence!", not one of them listened to me.

'Pop!' came the sound as they collided with the obstacles in their path. It made me shiver to hear it. Pop, pop, pop! And with that sound those delightful rainbow orbs – my brothers and sisters –– disappeared. They left no trace of their existence save for a wet patch and my brief memories of them. Was this the fate I had in store for me?

Soon there were just three of us left. We had already been through a lot in our short lives; we were maturing. Though we loved each other with all our hearts, we were aware our time together was short.

Just then my younger brother found himself caught upon a stray gust of ocean air. It pulled him away from us up above a neighbourhood chimney. My sister and I looked at each other and nodded "goodbye".

My sister and I were the most grateful little floating orbs alive to be able to see the whole world from up high. We could swallow in the land below us in all its most intricate details. I believe my sister was by far the smarter of the two of us. Whereas I simply enjoyed seeing all the colours and bustling activity below, she was much more inquisitive and speculated on the what's and why's of the world below us, which never even occurred to me.

"For a start," she said, "those shiny rectangles vrooming about and leaving a cloud of smoke behind them, they must be the leaders of this world. Look how the people are careful to avoid them at all costs. They must be very powerful to command such respect." I complimented my sister on her powers of deduction. "And another thing, you see those hairy, barking, four-legged creatures pulling about the two-leggeds by a rope? That means the two-leggeds are their pets. So, I suppose the hierarchy of this world goes like so: rectangular smoke-makers come first, then the barking hairy creatures, and then the two-legged pets, " she added reflectively.

When I asked my sister where that left us, for the first time since I knew her, she was stumped. After mulling it over for a spell, she began to respond: "I suppose because we can fly and none of them can, we must be the most important of all! But then again, we are not the only ones who can fl---"Before she was able to finish her sentence, a horrible squawking creature careened towards us and collided straight into my sister, almost hitting me. She popped!

I was all alone. There was no one left to make sense of things for me. I was just about to ask her what she thought happened to us after we popped, but now perhaps I'd never know.

As if to comfort me, the loving zephyr which had carried me along ever since I was first blown into existence, wafted me over the most delightful collection of sights. I saw whole fields of dancing yellow flowers, which waved to me as I blew past. I wended my way through dusky forest paths. I saw trees adorned with rosy pink blossoms, which made it look like the trees were blushing. Don't be embarrassed, sweet trees, I share your joy!

With each sight, I found myself growing wiser and more capable. I was no longer afraid of popping, for I now knew that just to have existed, just to have been a stitch in this glorious tapestry, was more than enough. I longed to share my newfound knowledge with my sister, but I'm sure she knew this already.

The breeze was slowing down. It took me to a flower-speckled valley at the foot of the down lands. All was calm and peaceful there, save for the occasional baaing of nearby sheep and the buzzing of restive insects. A horizon away, the sun was beginning to set. I wondered if the sun was a bubble, too. It certainly looked like one.

Softly, with the lightest of touches, the breeze which had shepherded me all this way, deposited me upon a dewy blade of grass in the ample shade of a willow tree. Here I watched the sky purple, the distant hills darken, and the sun set. Only after that bright red bubble completely disappeared did I finally allow myself to pop.

I don't know what it was I was afraid of. It was fun being a bubble, and I learned so much, but popping is the best thing that ever happened to me! I am now everywhere at once. What was the word my sister used again…? Oh, I remember: I am omnipresent.

When I popped, my body dissolved into the grass, into the air, into the land and seas, and into the atmosphere. Now I can see it all with my own eyes. All the beautiful sights the world can offer are right there in front of me, and there are ever so many! I am part of the beauty!

I was even finally able to go back and thank that joyful little girl who had breathed life into me, though I don't think she heard me. Most importantly of all, I got to re-join my siblings again, and a lovelier bunch of bubbles you could never meet. Sure, we squabble and fight on occasion, but it's obvious how much we adore each other.

So, to all the other new-born bubbles reading this, I just want to give you a word of advice to help you along your way: your life will be full of confusion at first. You will feel like a very small being in a very large world. But if you let this fear consume you too much, you may be unable to appreciate the wealth of wonderful experiences and beauty before you.

No matter when you pop, just be thankful that you were blown into life at all, for your being here has made the world just that bit more magical!

By Simon Maxwell-Stewart (2016)

Illustrated by Monique Pihl (2017)

WEBSITES:

Jesse Ward is the amazing Professional Bubbleologist featured in this book. She is dedicated to creating magical and memorable bubble experiences for both adults and children.
www.bubbleplay.co.uk

We acknowledge and thank Tom Noddy, the first bubbleologist, whose childlike sense of wonder, and intellectual and scientific interest in soap bubbles lead to the creation of this breath-taking bubble performance art.
www.tomnoddy.com

www.guinnessworldrecords.com

www.scifun.chem.wisc.edu/HomeExpts/SOAPBUBL.html Floating Soap Bubbles

www.sciencenewsforstudents.org/article/blowing-bubbles-science

Kay Tang. The Use of Bubbles for Breathing Exercises. Healthy Living
www.healthyliving.azcentral.com/use-bubbles-breathing-exercises-19405.html

Recommended Reading

If you enjoyed taking your first steps into the world of Bubbleology and would like to become a professional we recommend looking in to the more comprehensive version of this book called
Professional Bubbleology - The Art of Blowing Bubbles.

For quality bubble mixtures and other bits and bobs we recommend
Uncle Bubble products.

PHOTOGRAPHS:

All Photographs property of JWS Europe Ltd. except for where stated otherwise.
Adobe Stock Image.
All Historical Paintings under Creative Commons License

All copyrights and trademarks reserved to JWS EUROPE LTD

All rights reserved. This book or any portion thereof may not be reproduced or used in any manner whatsoever without the express written permission of the publisher except for the use of brief quotations in a book review.